No Hiding

from the woman in the moon

No Hiding

from the woman in the moon

Bruce Pascoe

This is a Magabala Book

Leading Publisher of Aboriginal and Torres Strait Islander Storytellers.

Changing the World, One Story at a Time.

First published 2026
Magabala Books Aboriginal Corporation
1 Bagot Street, Broome, Western Australia
Website: www.magabala.com
Email: sales@magabala.com

Magabala Books is assisted by the Australian Government through Creative Australia, its principal arts investment and advisory body, and publishes with support from the WA Government.

Magabala Books is Australia's leading independent Aboriginal and Torres Strait Islander publishing house. We acknowledge the Traditional Owners of the Country on which we live and work. We recognise the unbroken connection to traditional lands, waters and cultures. Through what we publish, we honour all our Elders, peoples and stories, past, present and future.

Cover design and title pages by Mika Tabata

Typeset by Julian Mole for Post Pre-Press Group
Printed and bound by Griffin Press, South Australia

ISBN 978-1-922864-40-6 (print)
ISBN 978-1-922864-44-4 (ePDF)
ISBN 978-1-922864-41-3 (ePub)

A catalogue record for this book is available from the National Library of Australia

for Liz and Jaz

Contents

The Earth

No Hiding from the Woman in the Moon

If she has risen in the night
and you are by water
you cannot escape
the hammered gold tessellates
of her marbled tower.
Her filigree fingers search for your feet
feeling for the fissures in your old face.
You have known each other a long time
and she is saying goodbye.
Her gold
the coldest of kisses.

Ratchet

Can you hear the ratchet
of the man who winds the moon
patient in the darkness
lest she rise too soon.
Lunging on the mighty wheel he hauls her up the sky
through the ink, past the stars,
through glide of bat and owl,
he winds her and he winds her
cranking past cold Jupiter,
Saturn's gas and rings,
the flight of seven sisters,
and the mad red god of Mars.
The clockwork gears
of the moon machine
slip her quiet through space,
but the moon man never tires
of her beauty and her grace.

Cogs squeeze kisses gently
as their greasy faces meet,
the lunar clockwork whispers
as you labour in your sleep.
Labour on, you common man,
sleep a sleep profound
the moon man won't resent you
dreaming on his round.

Transfixed by Night

Hoo whooo
somewhere up the valley
some dark tree
in a gully
tumbled rock
weeping ferns
hoo whooo
beneath the great river of light
the chiming ice of stars
the silence of dark space
slow step of heron
quarrel of bats
hoo whooo
calling along the river of air
sweet with pittosporum
that thick slow blood
warm pulse,
deep heart
hoo whooo
the low slow call
old as stone
locked to earth
and knee-deep in summer stream
a man
transfixed by night.

Saturday August 26

When you see the subsiding sun
lip and slip the west's salty hip
only those who have not kissed
will not move their tongue
and remember.

Only those who have not lost
will turn away before that
last ecstatic slide
has taken this night's last light.

And those lost will grieve
so deep within their coil
that their tongue is stuck
recoiled.

And for those who hold
of course your world is bold
and the leaving sun
a mere slipped disc
and the night a mild serenade.

Oh, leaving light
remember that I
was last to remove my gaze.

And if you return
I may turn away
your arrival no match for your leaving.

You saw not my eye
as I saw yours
you've seen it all before
but I, dying light,
kept my eyes where you left
the world this day,
and my life.

And the Earth was a Furnace

The stone was boiling
and when it reached the air it sighed
when it reached the water it hissed
and when it cooled
it growled and snapped
and became again stone.
The tempests, the deluge fell upon stone and scribed it
scored it, created runnels, etched fissures
telling the stone, you are hard, but we are persistent.
Making gorges
making canyons making rivers and lakes
great lakes
seas and finally oceans, where the gnawing and biting grind
where the deposition of sand
becomes a beach to lure the human
drugged by the dream of suspension
drugged by the uninterrupted sun
broiled in pleasure
and into ocean once more
for the shark and stingray
the stinging
the disguised stonefish
and then we weep and disclaim
about deception
about being hunted
the insult of another's power
an enemy at last.
And when old

and just ankle deep
we look past the waves
and imagine ourselves
as sand.

Blowing

It's the wind
tearing clothes from the line
scappering the bucket in the yard
pluttering the feathers of currawongs sullen in the trees
causes doubt
worries
argues with your thoughts
nyah.
Retreat inside, where dust on shelves
makes us yearn for the hills
where we are harried
troubled
mocked.
It is the day to reconsider, to test doubt
test faith
if we have no fear
and who says that?
The shimmering grass in wild ripple
that swirls the hill
the tossed ocean in the troubled trees
it is all bluster
dust and mistrust
yearning for the balm of sun
so still that motes are able to float like certainties
yearning to be deluded by peace.

Loss

If your chest quavers and you are moved to touch
which finger would you choose?
Well, take that finger
the one you would use to smooth
the mauve eyelid of a lover, the one you'd test for the
moisture between her lips, just before you taste
the temperature, texture and salt of a full loving.
Take that finger
with all its memory
and draw it across the
crown of this frail head
and watch the colour
ululate, a throat warble, a heartsong
as the pressure of your
loving finger depresses the napery of feather
let it progress
as a real lover would,
to follow the curve from scalp to nape
where the bones are tiny
so heartbreakingly fragile
that tears well in your eye.
Let your palm cup the body
the perfect curve of folded flight
the mighty power of feather and bone
yet the lightest breeze can puff them from a page
but merely riffle the page itself.
Lighter than paper
stronger than gravity
weather

destiny
fate
but your finger
can make it shimmer like velvet
whisper like love.

And love can be the reverence
of a wetted finger
or the regret of a finger stalling on the nape of a dead bird
but it is still love
and only love.
Some things pass
and we have caused it
other things pass and there is nothing we could have done.
So, love can be regret
but regret is always love
regret that the bird is gone
disappeared
because we didn't love enough?
Or because the angle of the sphere is out of our control
also just like love.

Running at Your Stirrup

While riding through the western plains
in 1840 god's time
George Augustus Robinson
Protector of Aborigines
a carpenter, a chief
came upon a black man
a black man on his own.
That man of Corondeet
knew the horseman, had heard of his hat
knew he was the Protector
so told him what to protect.

Robinson cantered across the plain
the black man at his stirrup
calling to the white man
the names of all his country
the sappy wattle
myrniong
a line of hills
a creek.
He told him this, his protector
for who was left to hear?
He yelled as he ran
to the white man's ear
I am the last of my people
I need none to look out for me
but this is our land,
who look after she?

Bronte Babes

For Julie who was there and Jazlyn who wasn't

All in hot pink
all in a line
all being taught
by lifesavers
to dive into the tidal pool at Bronte.
All brave
all different
all white.
Oh, little sweethearts
when you dream
of the gorgeous pool of privilege
this wonderful declaration
of Australianness,
is there one of your beautiful faces
that will crease, ever so slightly
and wonder
about the black babes
who swam there?
Where are they now?
Why do they no longer
come to be babes at Bronte?
If none of you lets that cloud
cross your conscious thought
we are truly barbarians
smug, coddled, selfish
a privilege even hot pink
and innocence
cannot conceal.

Written after Melbourne's *The Age* refused the essay they commissioned for Australia Day because I had ignored Cook's Enlightenment, the same day that a hundred children swam at Bronte in hot pink with an innocence which still cripples this nation.

Watchtower Picnics

For Johnboy Clarke

Quinces, warmed by the dozing sun
Corangameet.
Apples guarded by the brightwatch of magpies
Dreeite.
We picnic lightly
in the camps of death
wanoong.
We two, divided by blood
step on the stones of volcanic fruit
erupted from basaltic rift.
Yours, the story of Buninyong and Terrinallum
feuding over woman
warrior wounds cloven in quartz
a caution to us all.
Yours to tell
of the watchtower
between the mounts
vigilant for black.

Thieves still build towers
to watch the stolen
that obsessive survey
of the unwanted.
Your grandfather gave you stories
that only you can tell.
My burden is the tower builders' language
to plead for patience
offer the promise of mountain picnics
spread in the shade of wild fruits
should they ever turn their watchtower timbers
into garden gates.

Groove

He must have lifted his head
looked back at the axe
in his hand,
felt the edge
turned to the horizon where trees dipped to sea
and he must have said
it is useless
it is over.

The heart is just a dumb muscle
electricity in the nerve says pump
and it pumps
reliable as a Ronaldson and Tippett
steady, dumb, resolute.
We say it feels because we're looking
for the centre
something that is not the mind
or the hand.

Not the hand holding the axe head
forgotten in the groove
not the eye registering
the declension of land to sea
not the mind
with its need to explain
to deny, to resist
but the centre that brims
with the blood of hope

or deflates, collapses
nailed through the heart
by bone-hard reality
a reality it must resist.

At some point that poisonous vapour
must have breathed on his brain
stung it, cringing in the skull
withering the vibrant essence of a man
the pulsing brain, soured, corrupt and green
recoiling from the hot breath of gas
like the retracting horns of crushed snails
a gas that collapses the balloon
we call the heart
and that man, drawing his hand away from the stone
would have pressed it to his chest
because the pain there was exquisite
complete
it is over, it is gone.

Not one life, not one thought
not the groove in the rock
because it's still there today
but a whole orb
an entire globe of thought
the complete map of the known world
why stars shine
why darkness exists between them
why a baby is born

how to turn those babies into men and women
how to fathom existence
how to revere its perpetuity
and the obligation to ensure its protection.

That's the gas
that stole into his brain
poisoned the balloon's air.
I have not protected
I have not ensured perpetuity
I have failed
me
after all the methodical success
of galaxies of generations
stretching across time so vast
mud slabs are laid down as stone
mountains appear where none were before
deserts invade oceans
animals become opals
across that vast time, all were successful,
it is me, just me, it is I who have failed.

One tiny phial of that gas
and the city is dead
the city of the mind
of the spirit
of the soul
the essence of life that springs
a curled head of tight green from the soil

that directs fish to follow the glass wall of waves
that is there behind the mild gaze of kangaroos
all that
all that and the gas steals upon it
and corrupts.

The yam pasture is forgotten
the wicker gate to the fish trap
is ajar
drifting back and forth with each tide
mindless in its obedience to the moon.
No hand to slip the peg
that secures the gate
to hold the fish
so neatly, so economically
so necessarily
just a useless woven mat
drifting back and forth
like the thoughts of a man
who has lost his mind
no one to slip the peg of reason.

The forest creeps, but we are not there
to wring our hands at the waste
no one to till the garden
keep the forest at bay with flame since the time when Towerer
gave us fire from his tail.
No, too late
this is just scrub now, no garden

no copse of trees on the plain
for their artifice, for their glory
just a tangle of scrub we now call bush
and lie in front of bulldozers to protect.

Even the memory of fire
has been lost
the memory of the garden, where trees five hundred years old
are allowed to grow
for the birds
for the animals, for the fruit
for the simple grace of their beauty.

Gas, creeping gas
you think we just lay down and died?
It was the gas of doubt
the gas of certainty
it is gone, it is over.

Alright, alright, you say
are you done now
have you said it all
have you told us of our guilt
your loss
are you done,
is it over?
So we are guilty
are you happy?
Does our guilt bring back

the stone to the hand
the fire to the land
the peg to the gate?

No, but does your regret
recall the gas from the chamber,
restore the hope
rekindle desire
draw the fish along the glass wall of the wave?
And what have you done with the fish?

But here we are on the rocks
above the falls
and our reeboks
assemble by the grooves
our caps dip their peaks
like sad birds
to inspect the handiwork of great-grandfathers
great-grandmothers.
It is so close, you see
only several generations
since the hands that may have
slipped the peg
lit the brands
tilled the land
fell useless by their sides.
The feet here
shod in latex and nylon
the caps stitched with the names

of American baseball teams
are removed only a hundred years
from the hands and feet of the grinders
the peg slippers
the tillers
the firers whose bodies must
still be here, close enough for us
to feel the yearning of their spirits.

Is it all gone
is it over
if these feet
are back beside the groove
fingers sliding on grandma's polished stone?
Is it over?
Who said never?
Who said no way?
Who said we will overcome some day?
Will we do it with nicotine addiction
a delusion of grog
chuckling at the buffoonery
of TV champions?
Will we do it
by begging money
from those whose guilt we prime with a wicked pump?
Will we do it by painting up
and dancing for the governor
the queen
the mayor who is wondering

if we're really human at all?
How will we do it
my brothers
my sisters
my aunts
my uncles
my mother?

Shall we paint a flag
raise a tent
write a song
kick a ball?
How do you recall gas from the air?

My heart is with the man
holding the stone
stilled in the groove
a second before his heart
releases gas
because I'll never know what he knew
never even know the profundity
of pain in his stupid muscle
even though I've spent my life imagining that moment.

All that is left is the groove
in the stone
and the people's feet
three generations later
and a hope

a breath of will
not yet extinguished by nicotine
not yet harnessed to the begging wheel
not yet satisfied with laughter behind a screen.

Is that enough, my brothers
my sisters?
You've touched the stone groove
of your ancestor
you've glimpsed one second's worth
of his heart's desire
what is it you'll settle for now?
And you the alchemist of lobotomy
what shall you say of the gas released?
Did you invent Darwin
for this very moment?
Our latex shoes and our science
cannot hide us from the rock we forgot.

Namadgi

For Vicky and Frank

Gurrangoramba, tantanga, currango, yaouk, bogong, bimberi,
leura, orroral, gudgenbery, yarrbi, boboyan, callemondah, namadgi.
What did you say?
Brandy Flat, Scabby Range, Kennedy's, Shanahan's, Murray's
Gap, Kelly, Burbidge, Booth's, Glendale Crossing, Sentry Box,
Settler's Trail.
What did you say?
Two conversations separated by silence and gunshot.

Ready Cut Hut

Front door frames the end of summer
blond grass bent by the easterly
the alpine gums shining as hard leaves
sharpen their edges in sunlight.
Roos below twitch their ears, watchful, waiting.
A range, a dusty ginger road fingering the saddle crevice
the granite tors, the bodies, the organs and limbs
scattered as if in some old war
weeds trying to hide them, wind trying to find them.

Back door, service to cistern and trough, clothesline and gate
but look, that range
look, why is that creek cupped by her waist, kidney close
why can you follow an exposed spine of rock
leading from a liver half slipping from the cavity of a fallen mount
the habit of organs to collapse, and slide, to gravity's will.
Cast.
Look, look, all the fallen
all across the plain
shattered, strewn in grass that scratches above them
like a grasshopper's legs.
Stridulation they say
but we say doom.
In the slow war of earth
frost clasps boulders with icy fists
fires cannonades through the valley, across the range
giant detonations
cracking the icy air
explosions separated by centuries,

cleaving boulders as big as a house
and blasting one half-a-metre away.
Imagine the valley that night
frosty ears listened, noses tucked into tails, under wings
eyes bright with moonlight and alarm.
When giants are angry
creatures hide their faces
wish the night was gone
the sun returned.
But the battlefield is quiet now
while muskets are reloaded, jammed hard with shot
waiting for the granite to screech
the tension quiring in air so still
you can hear the movement
of the earth easing a limb.
This is a slow war
the fallen never taken from the field
their burial the mere shadow of a kestrel's wing.
And it's not over, for the dead are many.

Pickers

For Ailsa and her father of blanketed twigs. St Mary's

Seagulls in a shaft of windy light
might flare as angels of promise
but you, brother ibis,
still picking the colonial bin
ridiculed and rebuked for your hunger
stalk by the defeated Christ of
punctured feet, cowled and cold.
Are you there to witness his waking
or because neither of you
shunned, reviled
can ever leave your land?
Well, sleep on, fallen soldier,
step by bird of crust and shame
for the church is empty
the people on the street
speak with passion
to themselves.
Some must perform the vigil
to insist that humility lives.

Hyde Park Ibis

The Hyde Park ibis has a neck like a charred branch
hot coals glowing in the charcoal seams of its neck.
She flaunts a gauze of black Spanish lace
slipping fetchingly from beneath a folded wing.
The Hyde Park ibis was there with us
the day the old stones
of the oldest people
were put in our hands.
She will still be there on the day
we are allowed to lift them
out of the museum vault
and take them back to their land.
The Hyde Park ibis
is not a scavenger,
she's just been standing guard.

Owl

I woke when the owl killed
shriek of exaltation, relief
the prey screams in ecstatic shock, disbelief.
Two voices in the night
the code of silence breached
by pincered talon
stripped by beak.
One eye doused
the other ignites.
I lick my teeth,
clench my hands.
Cruel
glorious?
I scissor my teeth lightly
testing
tapping the microphone for voice
testing, testing
one, two, me.

Three Salt Rivers
Ngurkawamba Kunjim Kiah

with Dulumunmun

Wallagaraugh, Jinoor, Maramingo
Gwee a la, binyaroo
Dhang nudjum barkoll
Nyiroa, bunjil
Dhakabullitch warkbani dhang

Burbian, bura, googie
Bitheega, bimbla, bindhagan
Yuin munjaree
Nubiyn kanbi

Dyara dhakbatch nubiyn,
Wallagaraugh Jinoor Maramingo

(Stingray, cormorant, swimming in the water,
Bunjil and sea eagle, climbing in the sky,
mullet bream and garfish, oyster, bimbla and mussel,
Yuin people eating by the bright fire,
stars shining bright.)

Adelaide

Sand is what stone becomes
stone is what sand becomes
a sandstone city is what man becomes
waiting to become sand again
and that sand awaits
the compression
to become stone
again.
We are largely irrelevant
just building materials or decay
depending on the timing.

Her People

The Bread and Pomegranates of Kyrgyzstan

For the Samaritans of Kyrgyzstan and Tajikistan

Abandoned in Delhi
one air flight short of Guwahati
the terminal marble floor and perpetual ceiling pigeons
combined to echo their disdain:
You are foreign and we do not care.
Beg for a ticket
hard as you might
the pigeons fly in circles
and shit where they like.
But other foreign eyes
were there to notice
and motioned to me
Sir, sir, come
and they offered
a third of a pomegranate
and a small bread
please eat sir,
we bring all the way from Kyrgyzstan,
oh, I forgot, the pomegranate is from Tajikistan.
So where is the despair
when foreign eyes notice and have enough pride
and the sudden awareness
that even you from the west need their food and care.
It is their country they put in your hand
the pillow of dough
and the sweet blood of fruit.

Georgetown

March 1999

Here they are idling over coffee
nodding over the news in their mild town
fooling about with bits of keel and gunwale
pretending they're going to paint it.
Any minute now.

The estuary air is still
a balm
the seabirds too tubby to regard
oysters with anything but
futures speculation.

In the historic homestead
a cultured hand reaches
to snip a rosebud
where an archway enters a courtyard
and you might take tea.
Why not?
Tiffin is a nice word
for a rich English cup
in a still arbor
drugged with honeysuckle and ginger.

How could they
the people who created the beauty of these windows
the languor of these lawns
the bird-limed jetties
the sedate and seemly shops of the town
where gentle women

pearl and plain
meet harmless others
over mugs of coffee
innocent of any beans.
How could they turn a blind eye
skewered so willingly with their own needle
the wool from their superior sheep
how could they dismiss the lost
with perfumed lace flicked
from a scornful hand?

In such a gentle land,
suckled by all that is good
blessed with all that brings happiness
pasture, boats, oysters, beaches, slack water
an estuary warm as blood.
How could they?
Well, you can't blame
the horse leaning serene over the fence
the girl serving coffee trying to smile
without showing the wires on her teeth
the loitering boy scuffing his school shoes
not their fault
is it?
So, what to do
oh me, oh my
such a sorry thing when others die.

But you've felt the Triabunna ghosts, don't tell me you haven't.
A mullet slaps the water
where's the spear for that?
The oysters at low tide
are slicked with oil and industrial fouls
so even the fishiest fisherman declines.
Ducks skim at sunset
to the sacred backwater
where flounder regard the sky
with a double eye
whose are these things
who gave them to you?
You know what the oystercatcher cries
why the flounder waits
why the smoke of forests
hangs in the air.
It is not yours
even if her portrait sits on your shelf
because the paint is not yet dry
always slow when the dark has been overpainted with rose.
There's a problem here
for the old ladies
of teacup and shawl
the kindly puffed scone faces
hands gentle with babes and lambs
there's a problem here
not beyond reason
but well beyond reach
for those without memory

of ancestors before sheep.
But we have to accept facts
the Blacks already have
it's the ladies and lazy boys
the braced girls and tired sailors
who have to lay the ghosts
never at peace even by such sublime seas as these
that slim hand reaching for the foreign flower
a pale and graceful search for the rose
is not received by the land
with anything more than
resigned detachment.
Look into her face
and read her past loves
she doesn't insult you with that memory,
how could she, you weren't even born
when she was a full woman.
The jealous can never rest.
Rest.
To fall into her guiltless embrace
is what you crave
so look at her face
be brave, be brave.
Love her and learn her, cradle to grave,
for she is spread for you,
she waits,
not to rent or loan,
but consume you,
tendon and bone.

Moonbirds

Ten million moons
ten million moonbirds
ten million cresting waves
two hundred years to see them break.

We wait, we wait
on the shoreline,
we look south
for wings on the water
moons on their backs.

We welcome you moonbird
we call you back
to the strait between the islands
and the islands in the strait.

Come back moonbird, come back seal,
come back the people,
and the whales of their souls,
we wait here
on the headland,
we wait on the beach,
for the skim of your wing
and the keen of your hearts.

You cover the ocean
with your loose black shawl,
a net for the springtide
black lace for your caul.

Come back moonbird
to the ancestral shore,
two peoples await you
silent, in thrall.

The killing days are over
a new season begins
bring us your chickens, bring us your kin.

We wait on the headlands,
we wait on the beach,
shoulder to shoulder we face the deep south,
bring us your black gauze,
vast nets on the sea,
the moon on your backs
and your breasts to the wave.

The killing days are over
the rest to begin
come back moonbirds
all of us are kin.

Carrying the Goose

For Wayne

Carrying the goose
my cousin gave me
only three days old
the cousin, not the goose.
Just met and he says his family name,
I said that's our name.
So, cousins
and then the goose
lugged around in his chiller bag
motel room,
gate lounge,
taxi,
toilet floor,
we go everywhere together.
And I suspect the two cousins are about to be
the same.

Bow

This boy learnt wonder,
cradled between the thighs of the bow,
his ear rocked to sleep by a placid sea.
The world was huge and warm,
smelt of salt,
the swampiness of thighs.
He listens to the sea,
the familiar slap,
kittens' paws,
low tiger growls,
eyes wide to memory,
tongue numb and dry,
but adrift on an endless sea.
There is nothing for it now
but to wait for the grind of bow
on the coarse sand,
of an unwelcoming shore.

Kuller Kullup

Kuller Kullup walked
from the stony shoulder of Tarangil
to this bend of Birrarung,
spoke to all the people gathered there,
Wathaurong, Bunurong, Maap,
Wurunjeri, Ganai, Taungurong,
all the people
and he said
the sky is falling in,
bring me poles, the longest poles
bring me axes of sharp edged greenstone
for the sky is falling in.
The missionary arrived, as they usually do,
but Kuller Kullup refused to speak
while the man of god was there,
for these were the great seer's people
and his message to them was
the sky is falling in
bring me axes, bring me poles
together we repair the rent
in our world.
Of course, the missionary
demanded to know what was said,
as they usually do,
and for the price of a loaf of bread
to a hungry man,
and a blanket,
to a woman whose child was cold,
he purchased the information

that the sky was falling in.
Oh, those natives,
those children,
their savage superstitions,
Henny Penny, the sky is falling in,
and soon the whole of Bearbrass
was chortling at the foolish blacks.
Some guessed, as some do, that the need for poles and axes
had a more metaphoric intent,
a more tactical thrust,
and they made sure that,
Kuller Kullup, sky master,
dream master
was never seen again,
just in case.
How dare he assume a superior dream.
And so, the dust was settled,
the gold was won,
the sheep were shorn,
banks were vaulted,
parliaments raised.
Of course, the gardens
followed the rule of Kew, as you do,
no natives of course, no natives at all,
for nothing in this land
could please an Englishman's hall,
except of course, the grass and gold, the beaches,
a sunrise or two,
the quaintness of the kangaroo,

the docility of koala and wombat,
the duck-billed Ornithorhynchus.
Exotica,
unnecessary really,
when you could have a fox and a rabbit,
a trout and a blackberry,
thank you, Ferdinand von Mueller,
creator of the gardens,
destroyer of rivers,
the founder of the real Australia.
Kuller Kullup knew the sky was falling in.
And it still is.

Second-hand Canteen

In the auction room of old loves
the elegant vase requires
discerning antiquarians
to lean away, appraise
purse a lip, squint the eye
weigh the value, savour glaze
the cultured stance,
self assured
stroked in the hushed light
of someone's dusty trove.

The French lamp beckons a finger
to trace scallops of ruby glass
but that finger lifting the lid
of a drab and dulled canteen
withdraws in delicate disdain.
The lid falls on a pair of ruined spoons
last of someone's service,
hips worn, lips thinned, stem pitted and bent
but in the quiet velvet gloom
two old spoons cup and swoon
they'll not be leaving soon.

Scrape

Scrape scrape scrape
with dawn's hard bristled broom
someone's widow etching the concrete of regret
sweeping time to the clock of blood
but to all the world she is fey, is deaf.
Her teacups smeared with the scum of old lips
on the rim where the gold might have been
a biscuit somewhere
ah yes, this tin
a kind they stopped making
in thirties Berlin.
But a biscuit, a biscuit, a biscuit
when it no longer matters
what passes teeth and lip
you eat the biscuit from before the last war
a famine and a volcanic wave
but a biscuit, a biscuit, a biscuit
in the house where the clock
is a hard-bristled broom.

Kelvin Road

For Helen and David

The house of teapots and wine
dogs in the sun
noses in the fridge
pots on the stove
a babble of voices
lifted glasses
laughter
bodies in beds all over the house,
part circus
part home
part halfway house
for half the world
and all drenched in sunlight
clapped by clean washing
sung by birds.

Leaf and Limb

For Mitch and Libby

Suspended in a nest of leaf and limb,
a gallery of tall trees
looming above a calm inlet
salty and swampy
haunted by eagle and heron,
bream and mullet,
two people pad the fallen leaves
the murmur of friendship and love
between them
and always the cries of other
coupled birds
descending from the trees,
settling on their shoulders
a cape of sound
from a much bigger song.

Two Sisters Singing

Garden Bore, Tanami. For Trisha, Patsy and Janey

Watching the morning camp
two sisters
sit
one begins to hum
the other sings
they both sing
up and down that wavering scale
the wistful
the old
commenting on some old thing
realised there that morning
and sung,
despite us.

Cup of Tea

Garden Bore, Tanami

Cup of tea
with two old sisters
in the shade
nothing said,
just the land ticking
and sighing
like a tired clock,
ticking off time
in centuries
with every staggering stroke.
One looks at her cup
empty
time has passed
another buckled hand takes it from her
returns it full
she nods
or it might have been a tremor
the bush ticks and sighs
tea is sipped
life is slipped
cup of tea
two old sisters
cup of tea
long time
but our time
our old clock.

Adam Clayton Powell

Thanks.

Yoorook Justice Commission

Natchatung nunga.

Black Wallaby

For Aunty Barb

I love seeing your face
wallaby eyes masked by fern
and watchfulness
or, in your human skin,
that look of hope and love.
It lifts me, aunt,
and there are times
when the job of lifting is Herculean
but you do it with a smile,
just a smile.
We love you, aunt,
you make the timid brave.

Goodbye

Goodbye Sunny Boy
Ginger Meggs you larrikin rascal
you cartoon, you myth
you never were
and now cannot be.
Out of your loveable tousled shadow lurches
the grown Australian man
the practical, no-nonsense man
the hater, the sneerer
the booer hidden in the crowd.
Goodbye Sunny Boy
see you later Meggsy mate
it was reassuring to think
you might have been us
but no,
the casual waterhole poisoner
is our official representative.
No jolly larrikin about him
just hatred, contempt, selfishness;
RIP Ginger.

Duck-egg Blue

Duck-egg blue
diagonal straps
gathered at a bow
fitted
zipped at back
pink roses on blue ground
and other flowers, more rare, loose splashes of cyclamen
a drop earring of iced amethyst plastic glass
butterfly crocodiles clamp the dark coppered hair
an upper arm as lush as mango
a woman shaped as all woman
but,
rocking back and forth in her chair
like a catatone
slightly
but metronomic
the warning tic
and then the profile revealed
and there they are
hard and hunted eyes,
addict panic
unhinged vigilance
a woman
complicated
fervent or fevered
presses a water bottle to her brow
closes her eyes as if wounded
sips as if reluctant to be salved
a mystery like all people

gorgeous
desired
tender with the knowing
toughened like steel
but betrayed
by creases of flesh
where arm joins pit
neck joins blade
creases that began their fold
when she was first swaddled in cloth.
Fascinating
dangerous
glorious landmine
on which you willingly tread
for one catastrophic flash.

Beached

For Ailsa

The wings of family
will fold around
the tiny bones
of the beach washed bird
home at last
to the final sand.

Such a frail and whistling cage
to contain a spirit
so valiant
it would bare the warm feathers
of its breast
to the world's storm.

The beach was always your summer sanctuary
now here it is again
golden calm
spirits' balm.

Rest here, still bird
no more heroic flight
your small pearly innocence
here for the child's wonder.

If a Bird

For Mary

If a bird on a high branch
catches the last of the sun
on its breast,
is it as warmed as me
who saw the flare of sun
on that proud chest.
And Mary, who kept such vigilance
on pulse and light,
I wish you warmth tonight.

With Rinsed Moon

For Mary and Julie

With rinsed moon and sluiced stars
the seeping earth
the sodden forest listens after rain
the doleful plink of plenty.

Your blood they say
has glued, betrayed
but your tongue remembers
verse
so even while your eyes are closed
move the tongue and heart
remember moon, revere the stars
moisten your tongue with rain.

Sacred Ibis

For the Bellettes of the Springs

The sacred ibis in the park
uses the crossing after dark
the Hyde Park ibis
careful, kind
always uses zebra line.

The ibis is a caring bird
brave, loyal, never scared
looks after farmers
looks after friends
especially little kids called Fred.

She knows this kid
what the doctors said
that he's tough and brave
never speaks too loud
makes his mum and dad so proud.

Fred's got a fan club
the Hyde Park mob,
some are people, some are birds
but all of them have heard
that Fred's their boy, their hero lad.

Get well Fred
the world is wide
the Hyde Park mob is on your side
there's dogs to chase
rocks to climb
waiting for you in better times.

I'm out on the River

For Lyn and the river and my final day

I'm out on the river
cormorants are flying in to roost
a heron stalks the far bank
and a whistler scribes the air.
The lines are slack on the surface
but one is being drawn
a big bream is tasting
feeling for the hook
can I have a little sip
a glance at the setting sun?
No, the line is arcing out
a tight and urgent run,
I'm sorry brother wa gal
thank you for your life,
sorry that your rainbow mail
is silenced by the knife.
Now's the time for that beer
three pelicans fly in low
all our company mirrored
in sunset's afterglow
I'm out on the river
the air is moist and dark
the oars are shipped in the rowlocks
glistening and slick
let me go now
let me stay
leave me marooned on a low salt shore
with the heron in her secret bay.

Humans

The arrogance
the humility
the love
the hate
the honour
the corruption.
Cradling the dog's jaw
allowing the baby to clutch a finger
smashing the girl's head with a hammer
for saying no
searching for the hand beneath the coverlet
because you love her so
delicately shifting the noughts
to your own account
sharing your thimble of rice
with one who has none
waiting an hour in the rain
to return a baby swallow to its mother
turning on the tap to release sludge
that kills every fish
when do we exalt in hope
when do we let it go?
Oh, human, my brother
which one are you today
and am I the other?

Their Loves

White Petal

Carrying a white petal
to excite the milky dewdrop
to plump the egg
to fluff the first feather
to spur the flight
to teach the lore of white petal
the exhilaration
the taunt
the tiny plunge in down
and then the nesting
the nurture
the thrill of white petal
jerrung jeerung
the beat of such a tiny heart
an unheard drum
that holds up
this entire country
jeerung jeerung
beat on. Beat on
a tympany
of tiny love
a mighty drive
translucent bone
and half a handful of down.
Courage and
continuance
a white petal
of desire
and love
of blood.

Pittosporum

The blunt flared trumpets
of pittosporum flowers
intoxicate the air with sweet balm
warm and rich as a woman's breath
against your cheek
your neck
and you do not recover easily from this swoon
worse of course if there's a moon
and the darkness is stitched
monotonous by owls
and you wait, night after torpid night
for the nightjar and the swift
mangrove heron
battalions of cormorants.
These are the tides of blood
and heart
the steaming swamp
of wet kisses
the tangled sheet
the nets of hair
and blame the sweet horns
of pittosporum
and their maddening flume
for it is impossible to think
such thoughts
without them
responsibility is theirs
they poison the air
with promise.

A Flirtation in Birds

So, let us begin
with an education in birds
because this is my wildness
this is my life.
You heard my voice when the channel-billed cuckoo arrived
like clockwork.
It is such a thrill for me
that wild call
it tells me
the original world persists.
The arrival of the yellow-faced honeyeater
is so predictable, so reliable
that I might merely crease the edge of my mouth in recognition
the first cuckoo I usually nod my head
the first song of the golden whistler
will make me search the treeline
for part of my heart depends on that song.
When the jacky winter changes its tune it is officially spring
so that news is accepted like white smoke from the chimney
but when the white-throated gerygone
spills its silver voice from the top of the highest tree
spiralling down like a falling leaf
well, expect me to be reverent for an hour.
And, of course, there is frog song and mulloway groan
and the call of the white-throated nightjar
will have me out of bed in a flash
to search for the swoop of my spirit.
It will be a difficult relationship
a man with so many feathers to fly.

A Lisbon Song

For Julie

A laundrified lane in Lisbon
where globes are rumoured for sale
but four small iron tables
and one of them in the sun.
Call off the search for
the cloths are crisp red gingham.
And we order rosé
why not?
We are students of history
and drank Mateus when young.
And who needs a globe
when you can sit in the sun.
And perhaps they won't notice
that our knees touch
and we murmur in English
for our secrecy...
But in fact we are on
her couch in the
Australian sun
she doing emails
me in thrall at the wonder of love.
But the Lisbon thing
is just a flirt of the mind
it could be Laos or Launceston
Paris or Perth
we blur into the shape
of each other
that is all.

Love in 39B

Waking on the long haul
earphones perkily askew
like a skittled mantis
realise it was *Traviata*
the lisping, wistful trance
that slipped between my ear and sleep
not the glory of the soaring
but your face rhapsodic
that first time I saw you listening
face uplifted, aloft
I could only watch
as you flew
and even then
day two
there would be no other face
between me and dream.

The Economy of Love

When you,
passenger,
turn to look at her
how warm and crimped
is your eye
how soft and giving your lip
how slow and deliciously secretive your smile?
I watch you
because, dear traveller,
I yearn to gaze like that
to love
in the economy seats.

Watch,
her hair is soft and sheened
the slight, ever so slight displacement
calling for the gentle
correction of your fingers
please, dear traveller,
yearn for that golden head
to rest on your shoulder
because without it
there is no love
just business as usual
in economy class.

Be Brave

To watch as dawn
reveals her sleeping face
is a renewal each day
of my love

To hold through the night
within the circle of my arms
is my greatest joy
my life

The stillness, the darkness,
the slow passage of stars
the creeping globe
draws light to the face
of my wife

Stare unashamed
at the quiver of dream
restrain the finger
would dare to trace
the curve of lip
to kiss, embrace

Gather to me fields of wheat
facet jewels, launching fleets
this moment now
all I crave
watch her sleep
be brave, be brave

Pulling Lilies

For Vicky

You and me
murmur distance
pulling lilies in the sphagnum moss
Mt Franklin morass.
Honour our land
with care
our shoulders brushing
as we hauled and stooked
the beautiful thief
and in my chest and mind
the booming power
of companionship
eclipsing discomfort
swelling my heart
and your small cry of despair
when having repelled the invasion
you looked and saw a new flank of insurgence
but we both knew we had to leave the swamp
and the marching army
because in this trackless downland
we must leave before the setting sun
made our feet clumsy bludgeons
to the rare moss mounds
the orchids, the frogs
the sedges and nests.
One last look we gave it
and left
a valiant defeat
but a lasting victory
climbing the hill
to the late sun.

Caress

That last caress
revealed by dawn
diluted by water
dimmed by steam
the clatter of keys
spoon on china
the grind of bus and train
slam of door, ring of phone
copier churn
keyboard clack
and then leaning back
suddenly
trying to recover the sensation of caress
your jaw gapes
of its own accord
the miracle, the old record.

The Grey Funnel Line

Watched
your shaded face
in concentration's thrall
listening with the heart
glistening at corner of eye
line of sun on lips
tiny bright beads at bridge
of tongue and tooth
as words mouthed
in reverence, reverie, memory.
And now to haunt me.

In October

There was the foal that came across a paddock to sniff our hands
but it could have been looking for sugar
the sea eagle at Whiting Cove on the Otway cape
where we were collecting stone for a fountain
but perhaps it is often there.
The whales off Baran Guba that rose beneath our boat
to gulp at plankton and shearwaters who seemed
quite undisturbed to be swallowed whole
and then spat back to the surface to resume a life only briefly
    interrupted
by a dark and roiling cavern.
And, of course, the other wind-sculpted cavern at the cape
where a different whale was being taught to swim
by a huge mother supple and graceful in her girth
and where a boy listened within your own.
The wattle bird at dawn whom we knew for fifteen years until it
moved
to other flowers, leaving its sister, cousin or brother
to command our verandah, but with a completely different voice.
There were flowers in Venice, coffees in Marco Polo Square
and then your trip alone to Paraguay
and mine to Spain and Portugal.
But your search for tiny footprints under the branches
snowing blossom onto your back,
camera and brush poised in wonder at the orchid no one has seen
    since Menzies
learning to wrap cucumber and catmint in curls of lettuce
standing by your stove to learn the secrets of honey soy
listening to the suck of whale boy at your breast

these are the leviathans of memory
and would not leave me alone
will not
and when you fell on your injured knee
they gushed to my throat
like whale vomit
bird song
foal's whiskers
potoroo feet
so I picked up my special bowl that you had dropped
and threw the pieces into the river
cast away a new life in order to hold the old.

Oyster

See the oyster
cupped in pearl
muscle and shell
bedded there
skin on bone
slippery, sliding
curve to cave
hip to home
face to breast
arm to waist
lip to tongue
nostril to hair
press and stroke
hold and heave
the oyster beds warmly
in the sea-smelling shell
and wakes to the wonder
of wetted salt.

They Gave Me Flowers

For Geoff Anderson, Stan Grant Snr., Roy Green, Jim Berg and Aunty Roma

They gave me flowers
and I took them.
Man with flowers
knowing straight up where they would go.
Brought them home
overhead locker
screened through security
I was bringing them for you, Aunt,
and I got my daughter
and the three grannies
and I gave them to you
daughter, children, flowers, the keys that unlocked
the ninety-six-year-old door.
We come from stage people, Bruce.
Stage people?
Theatre, Bruce,
the Sharmans.
Sharmans?
Well, one was theatre
the other was just theatrical
show folk
boxing tents.
Black.
White side too,
respectable.
But all those years
all those questions
all the sneakin' about
trying to prise the door

when all the time
the key was
flowers and daughter
grandchildren
latest baby on her knee.
We're Sharmans, Bruce,
we're back.

Sitting

For Nadia

We sat together on a small seat
so small our bums had to cling
like frogs' toes.
It will be alright
she said
it will be alright.
It wasn't, but I will never forget her hope.
She had her own frogs' toes
the desperation of grip
but we adhere together still,
performers
bums on seats.

The Autumn of 2018

For Vicky and the pardalotes

The net is cast
on palest jade
an estuary
troubled only by the mildest breeze
and slowest tide
the surface not rucked and tossed
but simply warped, morphing
the golden web
stippling shallows with a broad and wavering net.
For some people the trance of that quavering mirror
is all they need for oblivion
all they need to have them spellbound
calf-deep in jade.

And at the dawn of those days
the summer blue
is rinsed cool
a lemon sky at dawn
tart, restrained, polite.

The swallows gather and twitter
thinking of travel closer to the sun
where insects dawdle and stall
in languid air.
The sleek birds dip their russet crowns
earnest in delectation of the journey
their midnight blue shimmering
for excitement of the north.

And in the drift of attenuated night
the full-moon magpie
queries the stars
in modest chorale
respectful of the season, the stillness
but in the brazen, pragmatic noon
it is always summer for the
broad daylight corellas
the football crowd of mundanity.

Or you might accept a proffered fig
the sun-warmed flesh
blushing to be so ripe
so ready for the seed to be swallowed
lips and teeth and tongue
a fruit of autumn and readiness
the sun still fecund in the flesh
so ready to split purple to the lips.

But soon the bats are fractious
the last mean apples
withered now
barely worth a squabble
for the swallows were right, as usual.

Through sway windows left open
forgetfully
or in hope
amber street lights,

are fret by leaves
already in their mood of fall
another country's temper
so easily transferred.

And with time
even the bones of victors become chalky
victims of their own righteousness
they glow like spilt pearls
but who remembers those of the inconvenient dead
the unremarked sticks of the fallen.

So when a moon leans
pale beams through
the crimped manes of colossal horses
chests heaving
bridles ringing
the planet is colder
sorrows loom as shadows
on darkening hills.

Those without beds might yearn all they like
for swandown and sculpted bolster
but the mall whistles malice
and surly cats mewl
at their reflections in vacated boutiques.

Even so, the magpie
rejoicing in the prospect

of a season of worms
on a professor's lawn
will call well and truly before dawn
because a voice as pied and strutting
deserves its own curtain call.

Oh, for a plover and chicks
on a river spit
convinced by summer
that eggs will yolk
and globe
replicate the world.

But today, the city is grey with concrete
and the wrappers of fleeting hope
oh yes, the perfect season
to regret the absent sun.

And regret is as cold as basalt
weighing on you
lead in your mouth
acid on your heart
dust on your tongue.
Think.
Think.
Think.
Nothing can change
but think anyway
wander the corridors of regret

scratch your napper
chew your nails
it is the season of review.
The season of wavering hope
looming regret
the hammering heart of the trapped rabbit
moves no mountain
it is just time undecided.

The chough in the cooling season
finds the comfort of another's wing
clustered on a limb at dusk
bearing witness to night's chiming cold
the pitch of clashing crystal
but wing to wing
chests puffed for warmth
our garnet eyes shine
with confidence
that the sun
will greet us
the convivial formality
of our march across the forest floor
will declare our life, we live, we live.

The quiet reach of night's creep from deeper shadows
tells us the moon is no longer full
but still, a walk beyond the artificial ponds of streetlight
will bring you to the trees

where a magpie likes to sing to itself
in the smallest hours
a ruminative, speculative warble
a philosopher pondering
the progress of night.

I promised to write through this season
to explore the unexplainable world
and its inexplicable deeds.
I am bearing witness
for my love,
intent on memory
of our home
and our friends
even though some of those friends
may be made of stone and wood.

Here it is, a song of our autumn
a small passage of the world's
circuit through a family of stars,
holding the hand of grandmother moon
and you on a mountain
the same slice of moon
but an altitude away.

Just a poem, no match
for the magpie's song
its tree
or the stone which the tree's roots grasp.

Nene

Vale Nene Gare, died May 1994

She's dying you know,
the spirit trembling to
fade through the flesh.
She watches each of our
faces
as we talk
of her
fascinated
amused by our concern
observing us from afar
absent.
The woman who bossed us
and goaded with reckless humour
has retired faint and innocent
just the spirit left
a wraith over which it
is too easy to talk.
But at the end she grabs you
and hugs you, kisses you
'you've been like a sister to me',
and later I have to
take your tear with my thumb
and press it to this page
and this page will
become another
only you'll have to imagine
the tear
which is our memory
of you

our darling
for it's like we've
been in love with
you all our life
and your late kiss,
at last,
is terrifying.

Gillian's Wanting of the Black Square

The earth is not an angry god
she does not inspect our heart for judgement
the earth is a true god.
False deities interpret your dreams and find you wanting
interpret their own and find themselves supreme.
The earth does not care if we live or die.
If we walk upon her she does not stir
but should we lie down
she will allow the grasses to grow
around us, through, upon us.
I can walk with that god
I can talk with that god.
The earth is a true god.
It is the earth
in her turn
allows the sun to shine on us.
The earth is a true god.

News

I love thee
the news hasn't changed
but the weather's improved
and the home-town team is in front.

I love thee
and it's raining at last
but the crops are in
and the ducks have returned to the lake.

I love thee
the bushfires are out
and the trees are still sound
green shoots spring to surprise.

I love thee
no cyclones ahead
and the high tide is full and still
the green hills purple at dusk.

I love thee
the sun of your face
the warmth of your hand
simmers my heart as before.

I love thee
the newsreader is shuffling his sheets
but in one modest bed
two faces cannot believe their luck.

And Follies

Sagrada Familia

It is subtle, power
it creeps
Sagrada Familia.
The might of that mind
the breathless flight
the fearless imagination.
The stony grace, its stony face
the power, it insists on being built.
The grace
the square-jawed jut
the humour, the fey, the great
mind of Gaudi
strong enough to turn
spirit into stone
but within two hundred metres
five chunks of melon
are sold in a space capsule
of plastic
and that satellite does not
exit into space
it persists in the earth
indestructible as plutonium.

And within that cathedral
the product of the world's greatest mind
a girl is employed to cajole
tourists with cameras and money belts
to respect the foremost pews of belief.
Of course they brush past her

they have paid
to snap the breath of the human spirit.
It is so powerful, so strong
we think we can last forever
a plastic drinking straw in a plastic sheath
for our protection
and our fingers flick it from us
an impediment to our need
a monument to our greed.
Gaudi, why,
why with your quiring mind
you chose god
and those who chose him
will allow the passage of drunks
inside your flutes of hope
because their pass came with
a combo tour.

They don't know where they are or why
but neither did you my brother
your Christ turned the tables in the temple
but the shekel
is still strewn
your tickets sold
for cameras to hold
your grace.
And still the spires grow.

In this hour
we hold our breath
lest your spirit
be stamped
for approval.

Foxed

Silverfish mumbling
fretting at silver film behind glass
stealing the reflected image
hooking the ghost
the image disassembled
disappearing
pilfered
by flat fish
oblivious of us
except to steal our silver
make us disappear
outfox us.

The Rule of Bread

No pretext exists for the cessation of war
the United Nations has declared,
indeed all perfidy may continue as before,
except that the rule of bread is absolute.

Any soldier of any nation for any reason
may kill another being whether man, woman, or child
of any race or religion
at any time, in any way
while the rule of bread is observed.

The soldier gives the insurgent, traitor, infidel, heathen,
oil baron, border crosser, secret stealer, fifth columnist,
unemployed, political demonstrator or vagrant
a loaf of bread,
inviting the accused to eat the loaf, the whole loaf,
and nothing but the loaf.

Upon the expiry of the three days it takes to consume the
    loaf,
and some prisoners have been known to take ten or more,
if at that time the soldier continues to feel the same anger,
his knowledge of the prisoner's crimes remains as certain as
    before,
or he has not thrown a stick for the prisoner's dog,
married his sister, borrowed a pair of pants from his father,
learnt to respect his mother,
become fond of the curried chicken of his aunt,
or indeed, lost complete interest and gone home to mow the
    lawn,

he may shoot the prisoner,
no questions asked.

There will be, from hereon, no restriction on the conduct of
war
or the level of violence delivered,
other than the observance of the rule of bread.
Bon appetit, my brothers.

Pig's Crossing

Pig's Crossing, Maramingo.
Fish spear, the old people said.
The new people said pig's crossing
so shallow they could drive the pigs across the jungle stream
entice them with corn, dropping it all the way to Eden
like Hansel and Gretel.
Pig drovers
famous in the district
for driving swine across streams through jungles, across the grass tree plains
celebrated in the district for their pluck
and their luck at being Englishmen.
The Maap and Yuin and mountain Ngarigo had different luck
because the Pope made a Bull in 1493
a statement that declared Christians
had a duty to take the land from those who refused to be Christian
or didn't realise that Christ was so superior
to their gentle Baiame.
The English god said man had dominion over the earth
Baiame said you are the earth
she is your mother
treat her as you would your mother
not as slave to your whim
your greed, your ego, your pride.
Maramingo becomes Pig's Crossing
and the rest is history.

Queensberry Rules

It's hard to lay a glove on a white man
because the Queensberry rules
were written by the Queen berry well.
So, when in pain and frustration
lay the leather on your brother
because, punched so often by the slave owner
his brow opens easiest.
Yes, get stuck into your brother
or sister
say they're not real Aborigines
because they had a different father to you.
Lash out, kick, scream black murder,
but do not shape up to the oppressor
because she wrote the rules
no better just to swear.
Swear at the white man
Swear at your cousin with the car
the nephew who thinks he's good now he's got the lore
yeah, swear, swear, swear
because thinking's hard, sympathy impossible, yeah, just swear
who cares if the white man wins
just so long as it's not a black one.

Someone Near Bundanon Wrote

Someone near Bundanon wrote –
must have seen the clean rock face
looking down on the road
from where everybody would see it
and he must have thought
yes, I'll put it there
on the banks of the Shoalhaven
boundary of several nations
home of the Boyds
this iconic Australian place
yes, someone
high up there
probably hidden from the traffic
took up a clean Australian brush
dipped precisely in the paint,
brightest of white
careful not to smudge or smear –
yes, someone near Bundanon
in a strong, sure hand
wrote
No.

The Gorgeous Black Mess

For Ali Cobby Eckermann

This is B flat.

Like this?

No, next one.

This?

That's it, beautiful isn't it?

Of course, he's not saying his wife's just cleared out, because it's not her worry, he'll deal with it when there's time, when the army's back on the road. Besides she's just a girl, a girl with maiden fingers on the keys, her heart aswarm with that wonderful chord. Her school teach piano? Nah. She teach herself guitar? Yeah. And learning piano every time she turns up in a room with an unguarded instrument, a loose piano. Not many about.

She's a song singer, delicate songs, hold on to your heart because you know this girl's going to sing love songs, don't you? Yearning songs, songs that cry, and that's why she steals time with pianos, because nothing cries like a good B flat.

Hallelujah he teaches her, chord by chord, Hotel California, Für Elise, chord by chord, tear by tear, and he's wonderin' there, why it's just a fourteen year old girl, still with passion in her fingers and the heart to share a piano stool and weep, key weep, chord cry.

Oh, he's hurtin' that man, binding his chest to stop it bursting, stretchin' the eyes to stop the tears, wider, wider, dare ya ta leak. He doesn't want to cry in front of these kids, these ... injured soldiers of the people.

Not this other one either, the tiny young mother, fourteen when she had the little spirit girl, fourteen with a mongrel man who scares the livin' bejesus out of the baby whenever he turns up. Oh, shame, oh sorrow, oh what a huge heart this girl has, this girl-come-old-lady with the straight look and zero tolerance of humbug. I'm outa here, she said, and 'nother boy-dancer he turned up and said, Hey girl, and she said, I'm no hay girl, and he said, No, can see that, because I'm lookin' at you, You can look, she said, may as well, but I've got a little girl. I can see that too, he said, Alright then, so yeah, you're mad. No, not mad, just lookin' at you. Oh, look away then, don't mean nothin', because I'm lookin' after my baby girl. I can do that as well, he said.

Big call for a young man, he must have really liked that lookin'.

Two men, black black, oh silent, desert men. Alright what those fellas ... oh, it's hard to say this, what these fellas are doin' and why ... look, both those fellas, them brothers, their parents got murdered. Different times. Yeah, you gone quiet, so did we. What can you say?

'Nother boy, well he's a man, he's holdin' all these fellas together, but he got his own grief too. Cousin go an' top himself. He said to our man, my girlfriend pregnant, and our man goes, well they say that sometimes, but this time she really was, and he really did. Top himself. And our man goes, I shoulda listened and I said no, my brother, like you said, sometimes girls say that, and you're busy lookin' after plenty of our soldiers, can't have eyes in the back of your head.

And this boy's clingin', hang on, hang on, hold tight, let go and you're back in memory, and memory for Footy Boyz in a dark room, shrieking and screaming and terrible things in there, things that hurt, so you would cling too, cling to others you trust. Oh, he talk the talk, the boyz rule, the boyz kick arse, the boyz win, but he can't take his eyes off the girls either, lost in wonder, also fear, and I don't know what that fear is, but you can feel it like the heat off a manifold, it's burnin' in there, it's scalding, cauterizing. One day, one day if he's lucky, very lucky, when all the boyz have gone to mow their lawns, lodge their lucky tickets and pack beef on their gut, one day he'll need a tough girl say, hey boy you weak as piss, you big tough-centre-half-forward, you got the guts to run backwards into the pack, or is you weak as piss?

Take guts eh, tanglin' with a girl like that, but there's a room full of 'em here could do the job. If you had the guts. These are the survivors here, the ones with the wires that defy the fires, the scary girls, the tough ones that don't take shit ... forever. Got the guts Footy Boyz? Hope so coz I can see the kindness locked up in there. Wanna let it out?

And piano girl is still going da da da da da da dum, da da de, da da de, da da da da da da dum, da da da, da da da, da da de, da da da, da da de, crying out for a German girl she doesn't know and no idea the song is for Elise anyway.

Another one, the mad girl from the desert, beautiful, so beautiful, and a mind like fire, mind like a whip, and how old she you think? nineteen, eighteen? How many kids? Yeah, two. Don't ask why, don't ask how, don't ask survive, too late, she already has, full bore, hundred percent survivor.

Another skinny one there, pretty one, well they're all pretty ones, there's a loose wire there, goes to do somethin' and then stuck, goes to do somethin' an' then stuck. Something tugged that wire, but I can't see what.

Same with other one here, something went wrong, bad wrong, and the look in her eyes is way back in her head and there's no touching it, no one touches it except that baby of the fifteen year old mum, she sees that baby and soft doona comes into her eyes, but then if she sees you look, flick, and the eyes recede back into no man's land, no man's land.

Piano girl, crouched over the keys goes da da dum, da da da da, da da da da, da da da, da de da da, de da da, de da da, de da da. Slender maiden fingers crouched, stalking the moonlight of romance, the fear, the fright, the drifting seductive tension.

Motorcycle crashes, shattered hips, bad, ugly crushing busting men in this older one's life, and you look close and see the revelation that shit makes angels, makes serene nuns, lovers glowing with warmth, who knows, but she's collected us here, in the Victor's Harbour, to try and solder wires, take up stitches, resew a hem, weld the cylinder head, patch and stitch, the stern love of the poor. And there's another one there, a six-decade angel, immune system stuffed, and so the skin's like a girl's, unmarked like an angel's, but the shine of hope in her eyes is not from zapped immunity, it's just her, who she is. One son said top, she said no, he said top, she said no, and so it's no, one daughter went to sea and frightens the shit out of white men, as if that's her job. Not what every mother plans.

Da da da da da da da, de da da da, da da da.

Oh, the lush blue fecund pulse of that gorgeous black mess of night, creeping creeping, against any better reason into dawn, washing the Victor's Harbour with exposed rose.

Sandcastles

Build sandcastles, little boy
watch the seaward side collapse
to the tide's wash
build your sandcastles then in the air
watch the wind fan sand around your hair.

Howe Hill

For Steve

We came for a death
climbed the highest mountain
cast ash
reclined on a granite slab
our old faces tinted rose
pinked by a collapsing sun.
And for our mate, scattered about us
grey wafers for our communion
a slow recitation of the mountains spread
Tame, Tinoor, Kaye, Drummer,
Merragunegin, Coopracambra,
Yambulla, Wog Wog.
A slow chant for the steps
of each climb
the voice reading the country like a weary bell
blackfella name
whitefella name
his country
our country
drenched in memory
like the spilling sun
and tolled respectfully
by a loving tongue.

Permissions

Permissions have been obtained for the reproduction of all previously published material in this collection.

Loss was published in *A Line in the Sand*, Pantera Press, 2023.
Groove and Kuller Kullup were published in Guwayu, Magabala, 2020.
Kuller Kullup also appeared in the *Australian Poetry Journal* , vol. 7 no. 2 2017.
Running at Your Stirrup was published in *Bulayt Bulayt: Poetry in Four Languages*, Fellowship of Australian Writers, 2006, also in Five Bells journal, vol. 4 no. 6, 1997.
Watchtower Picnics was published in *Antipodes*, Phoenix Education, 2011.
The Rule of Bread was published in *Untreated: Poems by Black Writers*, IAD Press, 2001.
Howe Hill was published in *Australian Book Review*, September 2006.
Saturday August 26 was originally published as Saturday August 26 Figueria da Foz in *Cordite Poetry Review*, 2006.
Love in 39B appeared in *Cordite Poetry Review*, 2016, with a Hindi translation by Jasmeet Kaur Sahi.

Bruce Pascoe is an Aboriginal farmer and writer of literary fiction, non-fiction, poetry, essays and children's literature. His publications have won numerous awards including the NSW Premier's Award for Literature, the Booksellers Association Prize and the CBCA Non-fiction award. He is the author of the groundbreaking, bestselling book *Dark Emu*.